NOTE

You would not believe the interest there is everywhere in farts. Since my first two Fart Books were printed, I have gotten letters practically from all over the world, although the most have come from California, for some reason. And quite a few from New Zealand and Australia, or from "down under," as they say, which seems reasonable when you think about it. Anyhow, most of these people sent me their favorite farts, or ones they claimed I had missed, so in this, The Last Fart Book, I will include such farts as are fit to print, as they say, sent to me from California and around the world.

It is clear to me, however, that human beings everywhere have a great deal in common when it comes to farting, something that makes us, everyone, brothers and sisters for sure, all other differences aside. Farts could even be the end of war, maybe, if we were to really get serious about it. Suppose every time a person anywhere farted they would think "Peace!" That could really change things.

It will probably never happen, though.

THE ANGEL FART

This fart was sent to me from a widow in Lubbock, Texas, who says that she believes in her heart that angels fart. There is no fart anywhere like it on earth, she says. It is her belief that an Angel Fart is like the sound of a feather falling, and has an odor like brownies baking. How she knows this is something she doesn't say. Personally, I have no idea if angels fart or not, but it is not a question I am going to worry about. Seems like they might, though.

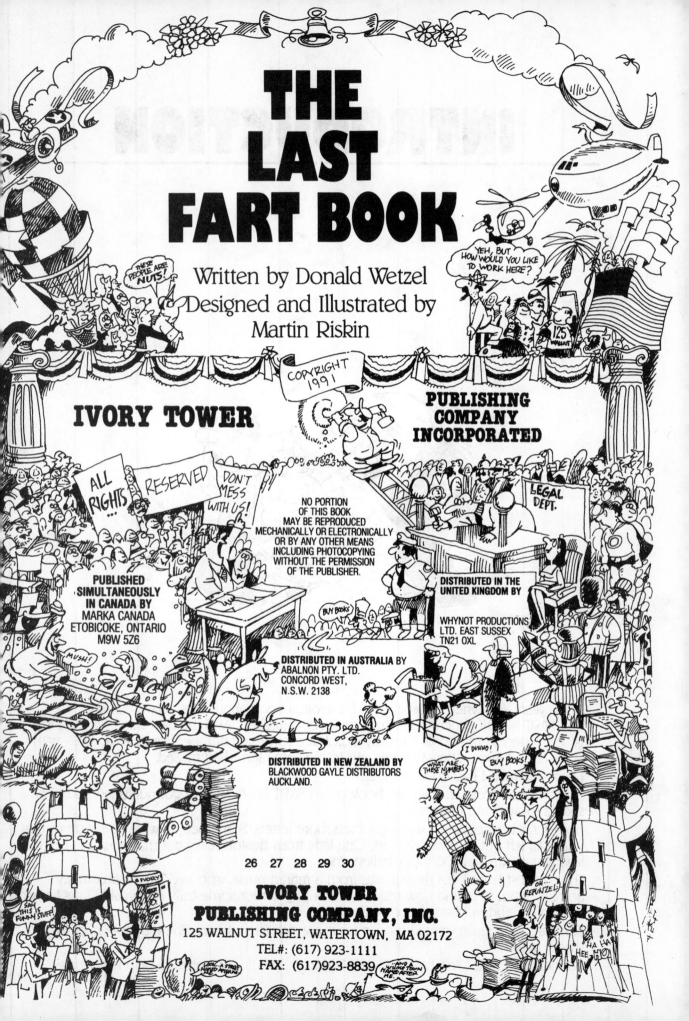

THE LAST FART BOOK

Written by Donald Wetzel
Designed and Illustrated by
Martin Riskin

COPYRIGHT 1991

IVORY TOWER

PUBLISHING COMPANY INCORPORATED

PUBLISHED SIMULTANEOUSLY IN CANADA BY
MARKA CANADA
ETOBICOKE, ONTARIO
M9W 5Z6

DISTRIBUTED IN AUSTRALIA BY
ABALNON PTY. LTD.
CONCORD WEST,
N.S.W. 2138

DISTRIBUTED IN THE UNITED KINGDOM BY
WHYNOT PRODUCTIONS LTD. EAST SUSSEX
TN21 OXL

DISTRIBUTED IN NEW ZEALAND BY
BLACKWOOD GAYLE DISTRIBUTORS
AUCKLAND.

26 27 28 29 30

IVORY TOWER
PUBLISHING COMPANY, INC.
125 WALNUT STREET, WATERTOWN, MA 02172
TEL#: (617) 923-1111
FAX: (617)923-8839

INTRODUCTION

A few years ago, when I was still a kid, I wrote a book about farts. It was called
THE FART BOOK. Much to my surprise it got published. And the next thing I knew I was
getting letters from people – mostly kids, but a surprising number from ladies, too, – with
every one of these letters pointing out to me some fart I had missed.

I never claimed I had done them all.

So, anyhow, I wrote another fart book called FART PART TWO. It got published also. This
should show them, I figured.

However, what happened was I got even more letters. Some people were pretty upset that
I had still left out their favorite fart. One lady from Boston really got mad about it. But her
favorite fart was way too gross, believe me.

The meanest letter I got though was from a retired nurse, who said I knew absolutely
nothing about farts, and how much would I pay her for some truly remarkable farts known
only to her and maybe some other nurses?

For a fact. She really wanted money for those sick farts of hers. Some people have no
shame at all.

But here it is, THE LAST FART BOOK. And it is the last. I promise. So help me. Honest.

THE MASSAGE FART

A lady in New Orleans who said she was French sent me this one. The Massage Fart is certainly one I would never have thought of, as I have never had a massage, but this is a fart you fart when you are getting a massage. You get real relaxed, the lady said, and you naturally fart. But you should not feel bad about it, she said, as this happens to masseurs and masseuses all the time, and it is their fault, not yours. I should think it would be okay to apologize, however.

THE MASSEUR FART

Again I have to thank the French lady in New Orleans for writing me about this one. (It was in the same letter as the Massage Fart.) What happens with this fart is that the fart is farted by the masseur, who will sneak it out while he is banging a person around and then when you notice the odor he will laugh and say, "Popped one out of you, eh?" Like it was his fault but your fart. If you are getting a massage from a masseuse, it is the Masseuse Fart. In either case do not be fooled; you should know if you farted or not.

THE RAINY DAY FART

I don't know about this one, which was sent to me by a girl named Flossie, which sounds more like a dog's name to me. She was pretty young; you could tell by the writing and the spelling. She said that on rainy days when you are alone, farting can be something to do, and that what you try to do for The Rainy Day Fart is to fart a real sad fart, the saddest ever. Like the weather, she said, only the fart does not have to be wet, of course. It is strange how some kids seem to enjoy being made sad.

THE TEAKETTLE FART

A lady in Perth, Australia wrote to me about The Teakettle Fart, which, if the lady can be believed, is quite a fart, and which should tell you something about Australia, in case you are thinking of emigrating there. Anyhow, according to the lady, this fart, properly executed, makes a shrill piercing sound exactly like a whistling teakettle that has come to a boil. "I have done it so perfect," she wrote, "that it has made the dog howl with pain." The lady seemed to find this amusing.

THE PC FART

Personal computers do not themselves fart, of course, but the people using them probably fart more than most people, at least while they are using their computers. What happens is that they can't make the machines work right and they get all upset and pretty soon they are farting like everything. The best thing to do is just to stay away from people having trouble with their PC's. A string of PC farts can really fog up a room in a hurry. This can be bad even for the computers.

THE SCHOOL-TEACHER'S FART

The thing about The Schoolteacher's Fart – which is any fart by a schoolteacher – is that it will get the kids' attention every time. Not a soul will miss it. At first the room will get quiet as a tomb. And then some clown in the back of the room will say, "Will you repeat the question?" After which it can take five minutes to restore order. But it has got their attention for awhile, at least. (The Schoolteacher's Fart was recently called to my attention by our home room teacher, Mrs. Schlotsheimer, who let one go that really brought our heads up.)

THE FAT LADY'S EXERCISE FART

Like the Coppery-tailed Trogon – a rare bird to be found in America only in the mountains of southern Arizona – The Fat Lady's Exercise Fart has a restricted habitat, so to speak, as only very fat ladies who do not like to exercise can be found farting this one. What happens is they are sitting down and have to fart, but in order to do it they will lift first one side of their butt and then the other, trying to give the fart some breathing room. This does not always succeed right away, so the ladies can really get moving around, trying to get their butts up high enough to do the trick. They can work up a sweat doing this sometimes. With some of them, this is most likely the only real exercise they get. Fortunately, such ladies tend to fart a lot, which helps keep them healthy, I guess. I had noticed this activity with fat ladies before, but I had not known that what they were doing was farting. But now I know.

THE VERY FAT MAN'S FART

This fart, like The Fat Lady's Fart – mentioned elsewhere in this work – is also a fart that happens in a chair. It differs from The Fat Lady's Fart, however, in that the man is too lazy to try and do anything at all about it. He just sits there with a patient look on his face and waits until he either manages to fart or he belches, he doesn't care which. Exercise and good health are generally of no concern to men this fat; but still I have noticed that a lot of them seem to live a long time.

THE ROCK AND ROLL FART

If you are a person who likes to dance to live rock and roll music, this is the fart for you. The noise of the music is way too loud for a fart to be heard – you cannot even hear your own, even if it is one that lifts you off the floor, which no one would notice – and everyone is sweating and stinking so much from the activity of dancing that the worst Garlic or Split-Pea Soup fart would go unnoticed. In fact, any time after midnight almost any of the more gross Rock And Roll Farts could seem like a breath of fresh air.

THE SMOG FART

The Smog Fart was sent to me by a person from L.A. who did not sign their name, just initials, and whoever it was said that this is a fart that is so bad it makes the air get dark around peoples' heads. This is hard to believe, but anything is possible in California, I suppose. For myself, I have to wonder about a fart so bad that it could actually shorten lives; but unless you have flown into L.A. and seen the smog coming up at you, you would not believe that, either.

THE LONELY ELEVATOR FART

It is a pleasure to receive letters about farts from educated people, such as a letter I recently received from a Mr. and Mrs. Groves (to protect the innocent, that is not their real name, although it is close), from Houston, Texas saying they are both fart aficionados, which was a nice way of letting me know that they were educated people heavy into farts. They sent me two new elevator farts, which was certainly kind of them. This one, The Lonely Elevator Fart is when you are alone in the elevator and fart and then at the next floor twenty-five people get on and they all know you did it. The worst part of it is that after that, you will probably see these people again and again on that same elevator. This is what happened to Mrs. Groves, anyhow.

THE ENIGMATIC ELEVATOR FART

The Enigmatic Elevator Fart, like the Lonely Elevator Fart, described earlier, was sent to me by Mr. and Mrs. Groves in Houston, Texas, and is, in my judgment, about as interesting and nice sounding a name for a fart as I have ever run across. With this fart, you get on an elevator and it is empty of people but there is a fart in it that is obviously brand new, and you will wonder how this could be, who could do such a thing and just disappear, even as you are also wondering if you are going to barf. According to the Groves, The Enigmatic Elevator Fart is always one of the really bad ones, or it wouldn't still be there.

THE GOOSE FART

A kid who lives on a farm in Gothenburg, Nebraska sent me this one, which I think is the only communication I have received about farts from the heartland, or from any person who lives on a farm. Farmers do not seem to be much into farts. I guess if you have cows and chickens and pigs and geese running around all over the place, a fart or two would hardly get your attention. The Goose Fart is actually a fart by a goose, however, and while I have a rule not to include animal farts in my works on farts, I have made an exception in this case, since it came from Nebraska. According to this kid, a goose fart makes a "whist . . ." sound, and is a very wet fart that leaves a stain behind it, so to speak. So it is probably more than a fart, but people in Nebraska who raise geese have a saying, which is, "Whist . . . said the goose and walked on," and according to the kid, this is the way a goose is about everything. He seemed to think it was pretty neat. For some reason or other, so do I.

THE WAITING ROOM FART

There is something about a doctor's or dentist's waiting room that makes a person need to fart. All those worried people being so quiet. Nothing happens. Everyone just sits there trying not to look at each other. It is only natural that eventually someone will fart. You never know who. But it happens, and it just makes things worse. This is worse than The Elevator Fart, because you are stuck there and whoever farted will probably fart again.

THE IT'S COMING FART

Two young girls in Scranton, Pennsylvania sent me this fart in a letter written in pencil on lined paper, and asking for a reply. They said that when they felt a fart coming on, they would warn their friends by saying, "It's coming!" They did not say if they always did this or not, but there are times we all know of when we wish we had been warned. So I would say that the It's Coming Fart is not only a good name for a fart, it is a good idea. Since the girls had asked me to write in reply, I did so, telling them that an interest in farts seemed to me a strange interest for young girls and had they discussed this with their parents or anyone? If they should read this now, I was just joking.

THE SPIRITUALIST FART

This is still another fart sent to me from California, from Hollywood, actually. Not to be confused with the Yogi Fart, identified in a previous fart book, the Spiritualist Fart is a fart by a medium, farted while he or she is deep in a trance and in heavy communication with a person who has been dead for thousands of years. Actually, if the medium is the real thing and not a phoney, it will not be the medium that farted but the dead person, in which case the fart naturally will have a terribly old smell about it, such as might be encountered deep in the Catacombs of Rome, for instance, or like the stink from a very old pair of sweaty socks left forgotten in a corner of a closet. This is for sure a very uncommon fart, known only to spiritualists and mediums, but it is something to think about, a fart that has been hanging around for thousands of years just waiting to be farted, and finally it is, and you are there! Boggles the mind, doesn't it?

THE JACUZZI FART

When I got this letter about The Jacuzzi Fart, I did not know what a Jacuzzi was, so I went to look it up in the dictionary, but the 1966 Random House Unabridged Dictionary, which is a very large dictionary, didn't know what a Jacuzzi was either, so I figured this was a pretty modern fart, maybe even a New Age Fart; but then I found out that a Jacuzzi is nothing but a hot tub with circulating hot water and bubbles being pumped into it, which means that with all those bubbles the only way you can detect The Jacuzzi Fart is by its odor, unless the fart is a remarkably loud one, to be heard above the noise a Jacuzzi makes, which is a little like a bunch of toilets flushing. According to the letter I got about it, all those bubbles in a Jacuzzi just naturally inspire a person to fart away, which is probably something that the man who invented the Jacuzzi, (Mr. Jacuzzi) never thought about.

THE HOT TUB FART

The thing about a Hot Tub Fart is that there are usually several people present when it happens – the hot tub being, so I am told, a very popular place these days for people to get together in a friendly way – and so the fart almost never goes undetected, as everybody there can see it. There is no way to hide the bubble it makes. This is where a Jacuzzi has it over a hot tub when it comes to farting in a crowd and getting away with it.

THE HAVE A GOOD DAY FART

My friend, Harold Tabor cannot stand the way people are always telling each other to have a good day. Harold is fat and homely and thinks about things a lot, so he knows that most of the time he is not going to have a good day. So what he does by way of reply when someone makes the mistake of telling him to have a good day is to fart. He will fart right then if he can, but he will not feel right about it until he does, even if it is ten minutes or so later. Then he will smile. The thing is, he knows that people don't really care if he has a good day or not.

THE EXERCISE FART

It is probably a good thing, but it looks like half the people in the United States these days are busy running around the neighborhood in their underwear or doing push ups in the park or lifting weights and jumping up and down in a health club, paying good money just to work up a sweat. There is no question in my mind but that this sort of activity works loose a lot of farts that probably would not have otherwise got farted. These are Exercise Farts, and are a natural part of being healthy, although I can see there could be a problem with this in crowded conditions, where everyone is tugging at weights and jumping up and down and farting. Which is maybe why they sometimes do this to music, to cut down the noise of all those people breaking wind.

THE BALLERINA FART

The letter I got telling me about The Ballerina Fart was written in green ink on green stationary and was hard to make out, but the writer said he would wager that here was a fart I would never have thought of, and he was right. "Imagine in Swan Lake," he wrote, "there is the ballerina being held up over the fellow's head, all stretched out like she is going to fly away, and she farts." That was all the letter said, except, "Sincerely, One Who Would Dance." I really get some strange mail.

THE DENTIST CHAIR FART

A dentist who lives in Marquette, Michigan, which I believe is in the Upper Peninsula, wrote to me about The Dentist Chair Fart. According to him, this is a very common fart. Dentists by and large are not known for their sense of humor, and it was plain to see that this dentist did not think farting in the dentist chair was funny at all, which is not hard to understand, as who wants to be a dentist in the first place? Anyhow, he said that he is convinced that people fart in a dentist chair mostly through fear, and if they would just try and stop being afraid, his work would certainly be a lot more pleasant. So I guess we all should try not to be afraid, as a dentist's job is bad enough as it is, just looking into people's mouths all day, and hurting them.

THE SNEEZE FART

There is a saying to the effect that the only really honest people are kids and very old people, which may or may not be true, but at the post office the other day I was stopped by a very old man I know and right there with people coming and going all around us he asked me if I had ever had the experience of when I sneezed it made me fart. Not yet, I said, which is the truth, and he said, well, it is a matter of our anatomy, as there is a connection of the nerves between our nose and our nether regions and due to that, a sneeze can pop out a fart that you didn't even know was there. No kidding, I said; and he said that, to be honest, it happens to him all the time. Which is being pretty honest, it seems to me.

THE UNDER THE COVERS FART

My friend, Harold Tabor, says that farts have a warmth to them and that on a cold night a few good farts under the covers will warm the bed up fine. Personally, I doubt if farting under the covers can actually warm things up much, particularly if the bed is really cold. Maybe for Harold. But what I worry about is what about if a person is not sleeping alone? I have not come to that yet, but I suppose I will, and what then? Do I get up and go somewhere else and fart? Or do I just fart and hope no one moves for awhile? Or do I just excuse myself and try to act natural about it? This has recently worried me some, just looking ahead. Harold says don't worry about it; worry about the bomb. He may be right.

THE POLITICIAN'S FART

Politician's are the only people who can safely fart while making a speech. They know it will never be noticed. This is particularly true when there is an election coming, and the politician is all worked up instructing the American people as to how it is that black is white and fair is foul and that the other fellow sleeps in pay toilets, and such as that. I mean, with this sort of heavy poo poo coming at you, who is going to notice a simple little fart? And you can bet the politicians know this, and fart away as they please.

THE SUBLIMINAL FART

According to a man who once worked in advertising and is now retired and living in Bucks County, PA, a lot of the breakfast food ads on TV, those talking about their high fiber content, are being punched up with subliminal farts – really just little fart-like piffing and popping sounds, the man said – to help the viewers understand how much this or that high fiber cereal will help a person go to the john. They don't come out and say this in the ads, but the subliminal farts are supposed to give you a hint. I don't know; the man in Bucks County seems serious about it, but he is retired and old and it is possible he just has a thing about advertising. Or about farts.

THE NEW AGE FART

Since I know nothing myself about New Age Thought I will have to suppose that the lady who wrote me about it from Salinas, California knew what she was talking about. According to this lady, when a bunch of New Age Thought people get together and one of them farts they all smile like there has been a communication between them which no one else understands. "They are so damn smug about it," the lady said; "as though they even fart different from other people." However, as far as my correspondent is concerned, the New Age Fart is just another ordinary fart. But who really knows?

THE OCTOGENARIAN MONSTER FART

To be honest, I had always thought an octogenarian was a person who believed in leprecauns and fairies, but I have since learned it is simply a person who is eighty years old. Anyhow, a person wrote me that he was an octogenarian and that he sometimes feared for his life when he felt The Octogenarian Monster Fart building up. "The Octogenarian Monster Fart," he wrote, "happens only to very old people, due to the poor condition of their bowels. It is dangerous, a truly enormous fart, and must be released *very* slowly, in drips and drabs if possible, for the risk is great that in just letting it fly, an older person may find that he has blown out half his guts." I doubt if this could really happen, but I guess when you are an octogenarian you have to be careful about a lot of things.

THE MARATHON RUNNER'S FART

You have seen all those hundreds of people all ganged up at the start of a marathon race, and if you have thought about it at all you have had to realize that here and there in all those half-dressed jammed-together people there will be a few at any given time who are farting. It just stands to reason. The trick would be to identify who it was that farted, as this is one situation where the farter can simply run away from his fart and get away with it, as everyone else is running, too, so who is to say which one of them farted?

THE BIRD WATCHER'S FART

According to my friend Harold Tabor, who is heavy into bird watching, The Bird Watcher's Fart is one of the most satisfying farts there is. This is any fart you fart while you are out in the woods watching birds. According to Harold, there are no people around to be bothered and the birds could not care less how you fart. So you can fart away. Harold claims that on a good day he has been able to identify as many rare and unusual Bird Watcher's Farts as he has birds, although I am personally of the opinion that most of the time Harold cannot honestly tell one fart from another. He just likes to fart a lot.

THE FUNNY FART

This fart was sent to me by a very young kid in Albuquerque, New Mexico, along with a picture of himself and his dog. It was a pretty sharp letter for a kid so young. "What is diagnostic about The Funny Fart," he says, "is not that it makes you laugh – a lot of farts will make you laugh – it is the strangeness of it. It hardly sounds like a fart at all. It can sound like anything from a cat in a sack to a motorcycle revving up, as the case may be. But every time there will be someone who says, 'Gee, that was a funny fart.' If you are alone you will probably say it to yourself. And that is how you will know." This same fart has long been known to me as The Mystery Fart, but if the kid in Albuquerque wants to call it The Funny Fart, who am I to tell him different?

THE PARTY CONTEST FART

Naturally kids do not plan a party just to have a farting contest; what happens is that someone farts at a party and then another person does and pretty soon you have a contest going on. Boys will usually see who can fart the loudest, while girls will try to fart the most interesting or cutest fart. Contests like this happen mostly at parties for kids who are not old enough yet to do other things. I have also heard that rock musicians will sometimes have farting contests while they are waiting to go on, but this may only be a rumor.

THE GOING HOME FART

This is another fart I would never have thought of, and for which I thank a lady who works in a bank in Opelika, Alabama. People who have to spend all day dealing with the public have a real problem about when to fart, she writes. People expect only service and a smile. So you hold it in until quitting time and you are safely in your car, when you will sometimes fart continuously all the way home. This may be a relief, the lady writes, but it is a lousy way to end the day. Which is no doubt true, but there probably isn't much that can be done about it.

THE FISH FART

Nothing I have ever read or heard about has led me to believe that a fish can fart, but a fellow in Moorhead, Minnesota – the land of a thousand lakes – says they can. What happens, according to the letter I got on the subject, is that there are just two people in a boat out in the middle of a lake, and suddenly there is a rotten fart smell in the air. You would think it had to be one of the two people, but to avoid discussion and possible recriminations one of them will say, "the fish sure are farting bad today," and the other one will say, "they sure are," and they will go back to fishing. Which is a sensible way of handling a fart between two people way out in the middle of a lake; but in my opinion this is about as phony a fart as has ever been called to my attention, although my thanks to Mr. Olson all the same.

THE REVERSE FART

This is a fart by a kid, who makes a phony farting noise to call attention to himself, and someone being sarcastic says, "Now do it with your mouth," and the kid holds up his hand for silence and then actually farts. Everybody knows kids like this. Anything to be different.

THE SMOKER'S FART

Believe it or not this fart came to me written on a post card. A person will fart and try to conceal the odor by lighting a cigarette. If it is bad enough, other people will start lighting up in self defense, and the farter may get away with it, as it could have been any person smoking. However, in a situation like this, the people present who don't smoke are really in for it, having to breathe in all that smoke as well as the fart, which hardly seems fair.

THE MOOSE CALL FART

The letter telling me about this unusual fart came from a place called Moosejaw, Saskatchewan, which is in Canada. It started out, "You have probably never heard the call of a moose in rut." Naturally you will finish reading a letter that starts out like that. I did, and what the letter said was that many years ago there was a French Canadian logger who could fart a fart that sounded just like the call of a moose in rut, and while these Moose Call Farts never actually called up a moose, all wild-eyed and with water lilies hanging from his antlers, there was always the danger that they might. According to the letter writer, a moose in rut could really tear things up. And so could The Moose Call Fart, it seems to me.

THE PASSWORD FART

Leave it to some crazy kids to come up with a fart as their secret password. The letter I got about this was kind of sad, however. The members of this club were supposed to fart whenever they met, this being their secret signal to each other; but according to the kid's letter, most of the time it didn't work, and they would just stand there straining and making faces at each other. There had even been a couple of accidents that way; but when it worked, the kid said, it was really neat. What was sad, though, was that the kid really believed I would have some great advice for them, about how they could manage to fart whenever they met; when all I could write and tell them was that maybe they should try just shaking hands.

THE FUNERAL FART

Believe it or not, three different people wrote to me about this fart. Everyone of them said they had been there when it happened. I guess you do not forget a thing like that. Still, if it had not been brought to my attention three times, I doubt if I would have mentioned it. But one of the letter writers said that the Funeral Fart he had heard made a keening sound so natural and sad that a lot of people probably didn't even know it had been a fart. I guess if you have to fart at a funeral, you should hope it would be a fart like that, and not a funny one.

THE UNFAIR FART

This is any fart that is used to terminate a hotly contested domestic argument, resulting in a win by the farter, who has usually been getting the worst of it up until then, and who is generally a man. Generally speaking most women, so I am told, even altogether liberated women, will draw the line at blowing a person away at the end of an argument with a fart. And thank goodness for that. But not so the man, I am sorry to say, who will fart to win if he can, no matter how unfair the fart, or how foul, which it usually is. It is my understanding that this is a fart that is way too common.

THE GREAT KILLER FART

I have gotten several letters from people describing a fart that is said to kill flying and crawling insects, house plants, tropical fish, cats and small dogs or even humans who are ill or elderly. "You have forgotten The Great Killer Fart," I am told. Well, if people want to believe there is a Great Killer Fart such as this they will believe it, but as far as I am concerned the Great Killer Fart, like the unicorn, is a mythical beast. In the real world, there is simply no such thing. It is true, however strange as it may seem, that if a person intentionally farts a lot around an African Violet plant it will actually turn brown and die.

THE FEAR OF FLYING FART

This fart came to me from an airline stewardess in Denver, and was on pink stationery with some drawings of the Playboy Rabbit on it, which makes you wonder. But she wrote that if people were afraid of flying she wished they would take the train, for if it is not fear that does it, why do so many people seem to fart from the time they get on a plane until they get off?

According to this stewardess, anyhow, it should be, "come fly the flatulent skies," sometimes. She also said, in a post script, that she would rather have several obnoxious drunks on board grabbing at her butt than one fat scared old man full of gas. I would guess she did not realize she was writing to a kid, but that is what she wrote. There is some drawback to every job, I guess.

THE FINAL FART

The way it happened was, a traveling salesman's car broke down and he had to spend the night with a farmer and his lonely young daughter. All they had for supper was beans, but beans were the salesman's favorite food, so that was fine with him. All through supper the farmer's daughter kept telling the salesman to have some more beans and being nice to him in other ways, but he noticed the farmer watching him, so he quit with the beans and went to bed. Later that night a storm came up and the farmer went out to see about his stock, and the girl came into the salesman's room and said, "Quick, now's your chance," and he jumped up and ran to the kitchen and finished eating all the beans.

The next morning he was out in the barnyard saying goodbye to the farmer when suddenly all those beans took a hold at once and he farted a single fart so powerful it blew the feathers off the farmer's chickens. Well, the farmer figured that any man who could fart like that was not fit to live among decent people, so he shot him. And not since that day has such a fart occurred again in all that county or anywhere else. (Naturally some of my readers will know of a better Final Fart than this, but this is *my* Final Fart. For real. Honest.)

IVORY TOWER PUBLISHING COMPANY INCORPORATED

These other fun books are available at many fine stores or by sending $3.50 ea. directly to the publisher.

2000-Do Diapers Give You Leprosy? A humorous look at what every parent should know about bringing up babies.

2008-Adult Connect the Dots. You played connect the dots as a child, but never like this!

2015-Games You Can Play With Your Pussy. And lots of other stuff cat owners should know.

2026-Games You Can Play In Bed. A humorous compendium covering everything from Bedtime Bingo to Things To Do at 3:45 A.M.

2027-How To Pick Up Girls. Bridget is back to show all philanderers some proper pick-up techniques.

2034-You Know You're Over Forty When... You Think "Grass" is something to cut and "Getting a little action" means your prune juice is working. A perfect 40th birthday gift.

2042-Cucumbers Are Better Than Men Because... They don't care if you shave your legs, and they never walk around your place when the shades are up. At last, ladies, revenge for all our male chauvinist books.

2059-Small Busted Women Have Big Hearts. Finally a book that boasts the benefits of being small busted in our society where bigger is better! A super way to bolster the ego of every slender woman.

2061-I'd Rather Be 40 Than Pregnant... Or worrying about getting into graduate school, or travelling with young children, or getting no respect at a ritzy store. Great moral support for women reaching the diaperless age.

2064-The Wedding Night-Facing Nuptial Terrors. For brides and grooms alike: What To Do If He Wants To Take Pictures; What To Do If She Won't Come Out Of The Bathroom; and many more hilariously funny situations newlyweds may encounter.

2067-It's Time To Retire When... Your boss is younger than you are, you stop to think and sometimes forget to start again, or you feel like the morning after and you swear you haven't been anywhere.

2068-Sex Manual For People Over 30. Includes great excuses for nonperformance, rediscovering foreplay, and how to tell an orgasm from a heart attack.

2101-Peter Pecker's Guide To The Male Organ. A detailed analysis of the types of men who own Wee Wee's, Members, Weenies, Dinks, Schlongs, No Nos, Tools, Wangs, and many others. Everyone is covered, from accountants to taxi drivers.

2102-You Know You're Over 50 When... You add "God willing" to the end of most of your statements and you don't care where your wife goes when she goes out, as long as you don't have to go with her. A great 50 year old birthday gift.

2109-The Get Well Book. Cheer up sick folks with this book that teaches them how to gain sympathy, what the doctor really means and how to cope with phones, kids, germs and critters that make you sick.

2121-More Dirty Crosswords. This latest edition of dirty crosswords will test your analytical powers even further as you struggle to improve your vocabulary.

2123-You Know You're Over 60 When... You're 60 when you start straddling two road lanes, you start

looking forward to dull evenings at home, and you can't remember when prunes and figs weren't a regular part of your diet.

2127-Your Golf Game Is In Big Trouble When... Your practice rounds are all in the bar and you've tried out 30 putters and none of them work and you play whole rounds without once hitting the fairway.

2129-Fun In The John. More fun than you ever dreamed possible. Crosswords, Bathroom Lists, Word Searches, Mystery Games, John Horoscopes, Connect The Dots, Mazes, and Much More.

2131-The Fart Book. Farts are divided into two groups. 1. Your farts. 2. Somebody else's fart. This book lists them all, the Little Girls Don't Fart Fart, The Dog Did It Fart, the S'cuse me Fart and many more.

2136-The Shit List. The list is quite extensive and describes the versatile use of this clever word. There is, for example, "chicken shit" and "give a shit" and "shoot the shit". A very funny book, No Shit.

2148-Dear Teacher... A hilarious collection of actual parents' notes to teachers. "Please excuse Joe from school yesterday. He had diarrhea through a hole in his shoe."

2153-Fart Part II. This sequel covers the dreaded "Thank God I'm Alone Fart", the insidious "SBD Fart" and the awe-inspiring "Sonic Boom Fart".

2162-The Booger Book. All boogers can be divided into two groups: 1) dry boogers: 2) wet boogers. This book covers them all, from the swimmer's booger to types of booger disposal techniques.

2166-You've Survived Catholic School When... You can enter a phone booth without feeling you should begin confessing and you don't shudder when someone hands you a ruler.

2175-Asses. The complete directory of asses of all kinds from the Male Biker's Buns to the Oh Wow! Ass.

2177-You're Over the Hill When... No one cares anymore about what you did in high school, and you see your old cereal bowl in an antique shop.

2178-The Pregnant Father. The Pregnant Father's chief duty during delivery is to hold a little pan while his wife throws up into it...and much more!

2180-Italian Sex Manual. Covers everything from picking up Italian men to great Italian sex games and why Italian men are better lovers.

2181-Jewish Sex Manual. Includes detailed information about what Jewish women love about sex, how to pick up Jewish men and great Jewish blind dates.

2187-Big Busted Women Have More Fun... Big busted women somehow seem more motherly, get the most out of stretch fabric and always know where to look for a lost earring.

2188-Great Sex For Busy Couples... Explains how to find the time, the place and the desire when two careers keep the couple running.

2190-Teddy Bears Are Better Than Men Because... They don't hog the whole bed and they invariably understand when you have a headache.

2192-You Know You're Over 30 When... You start wearing underwear almost all of the time; you find the first grey hair and you no longer have to lie

on your resume.

2193-The Bitch Book. The Bitch takes two spaces when she parks, is irritable every day of the month, and always goes through the express line at the supermarket.

2195-Beer Is Better Than Women Because... Beers don't want a lasting relationship, and beer doesn't expect an hour of foreplay before satisfying you.

2198-The P.M.S. Book. What every woman experiences once a month. Includes the Irritability Syndrome, the Tender Boobs Syndrome and the Chocolate Syndrome.

2200-Shit Happens... It happens when the IRS asks for the receipts, your husband leaves you for an older woman, or you call suicide prevention and they put you on hold.

2202-Stressed Out... Being stressed out is trying to enjoy a cigarette in a non-smoking office, or having some kid park your brand new car.

2203-The Last Fart Book. This final sequel concludes with the Under The Cover Fart, the Waiting Room Fart, the Excuses Fart and many others.

2205-Is There Sex After 40? Normal 40-year olds do it once a week. Covers everything from sexy cardigans to tucking a vest into your underpants.

2206-Adult Party Games. Many original and some old favorite "permissively naughty" party games that will bring a party together and keep it roaring through the night.

2207-Underwear. The complete directory of Underwear from the Old Fashioned Long Johns to The French Cut Briefs.

2210- Is There Sex After Marriage? This great work covers everything from faking an orgasm to philandering to excuses for more or less sex. It even answers the age old question, Is There Sex After Pets?

2211- Boobs. Using the Standard Boob as a benchmark, this screamer examines the Pillow Boobs, Star Gazers, Spreaders, Ninnies, Disappearing Boobs, Oh Wow! Boobs and 40 others.

2212- Life With A Sports Junky. The Sports Junky spent part of his honeymoon in a grandstand, still asks his old coach for advice and thinks sex is O.K. as long as it is over by game time.

2213- Women Over 50 Are Better... They can tune out the worst snoring, have more womanly figures & won't make you sleep in the middle of a stuffed animal collection.

2214-Is There Sex After Divorce? All the funny situations when a middle aged person starts to date again, from not fooling around on the first date to finding a zit on your date's ear.

2215-Over 65, The Golden Years? Great birthday and retirement gift. Describes "Bellies Are Beautiful", Early Bird Dinners", "Retirement, What Now?" and much more.

2216-Hanky Panky. Cartoons of the animal kingdom in their favorite amorous (and unmentionable) pastime. Brilliant full color drawings are riotously funny.

2217-Is There Sex After 50? Swapping your mate for two 25-year-olds, finding places to put your cold feet, and telling grandchildren about when you were a hippy.

2218-Is There Sex After 60?

Searching, in depth, cartoon report the sexual behavior and horrible ha of the Don Juans of the Geriatric se The Sewing Circle Seductress matc wits with the Casanovas of the Bin Halls.

2219-Crosswords For Shitheads. that person you feel is full of "it".

2220-Crosswords For Farters. A crossword puzzle book for people w gastrointestinal distress.

2221-Crosswords For Your Birthday. An irreverent crossword puzzle book for people who are terribly lonesome on their birthday.

2222-Crosswords For Bored Love Designed to test you and your partn sexual knowledge (or lack of it). Gr your lover, think sex, and dive in... this collection of crosswords for tho with a cloistered bawdy nature.

2223-Games You Can't Lose. An exciting way to test your skills and increase your self-confidence with puzzles, mazes, word searches, and many more games.

2224-Life's A Picnic If You Have Big Weenie. Covers where big weenies come from, what women li about big weenies, making a teenie weenie into a big weenie, and much more.

2225-Women Over 40 Are Better Because... They know just what it takes to make their man feel good an they can eat a double hot fudge sund and not worry about "breaking out".

2226-C.R.S. (Can't Remember Shi It happens to the best of us like forgetting the punch line of a great joke, where you parked the car, or where you left your glasses.

2227-Happy Birthday! You Know You're A Year Older When... You longer eat all the dessert just because it's there and you can no longer easil sleep till noon.

2228-You're Hooked On Fishing When... You start to raise your own worms, you visit the emergency roon at least once a year to have a hook removed, and you're on a first name basis with the Coast Guard.

2229-You Know You're A Redneck When... You wear bib overalls, eat grits, love cow tipping, and think a mud wrestling place is hog heaven.

2230-A Coloring Book for Pregnan Mothers To Be. Tender and funny, from being unable to see the scale to controlling your proud parents.

2231-Eating Pussy The Official Cat Cookbook. This book will not only offer you great new ideas for serving pussy to your guests, but it is sure to expand your recipe file.

2232-Life's More Fun When You're 21... This book humorously covers the trials of coming of age such as parenta trust, joining the work force, and balancing budgets.

IVORY TOWER PUBLISHING CO., INC.   125 Walnut Street, Watertown, MA 02172   **(617) 923-1111**